All About Me

Point and Say

All About Me
a very first picture book

HERMES HOUSE

First published in 1998 by Hermes House

Hermes House books are available for bulk purchase for sales promotion and for premium use.
For details, write or call the sales director,

Hermes House, 27 West 20th Street, New York, NY 10011
(800) 354-9657

© Anness Publishing Limited 1998

Hermes House is an imprint of Anness Publishing Inc.

ISBN 1 84038 157 4

Publisher: Joanna Lorenz
Senior Editor: Catherine Barry
Designer: Julie Francis

Printed in Hong Kong/China

1 3 5 7 9 10 8 6 4 2

Contents

My Body

Body

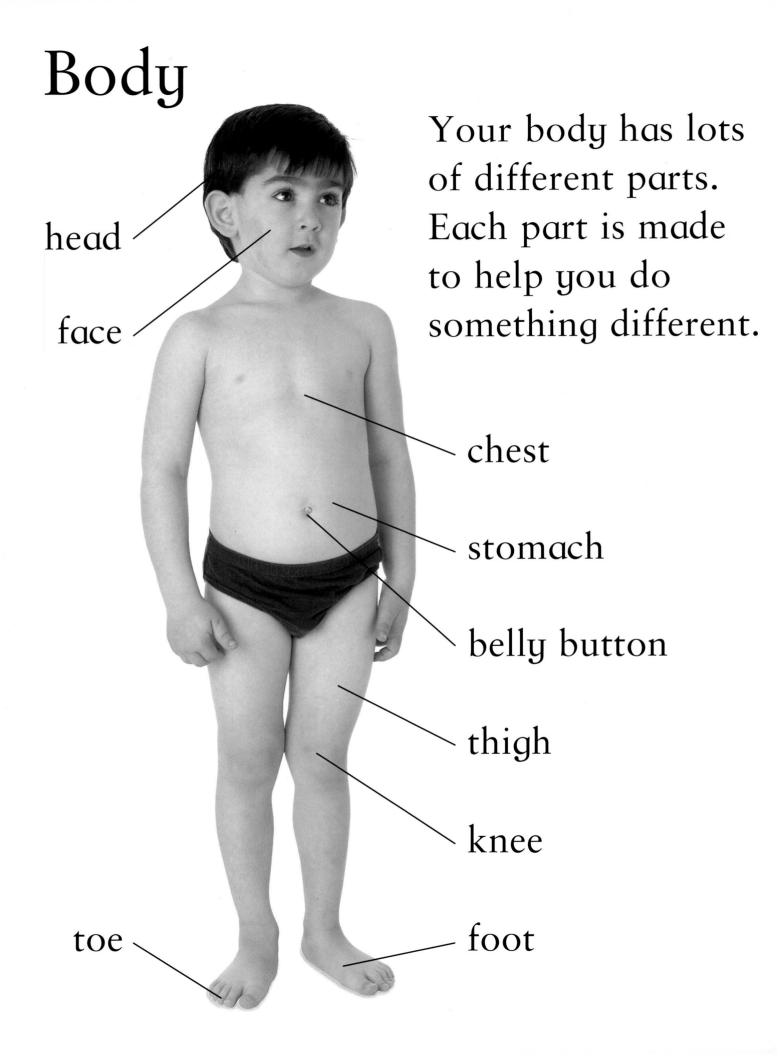

Your body has lots of different parts. Each part is made to help you do something different.

head

face

chest

stomach

belly button

thigh

knee

toe

foot

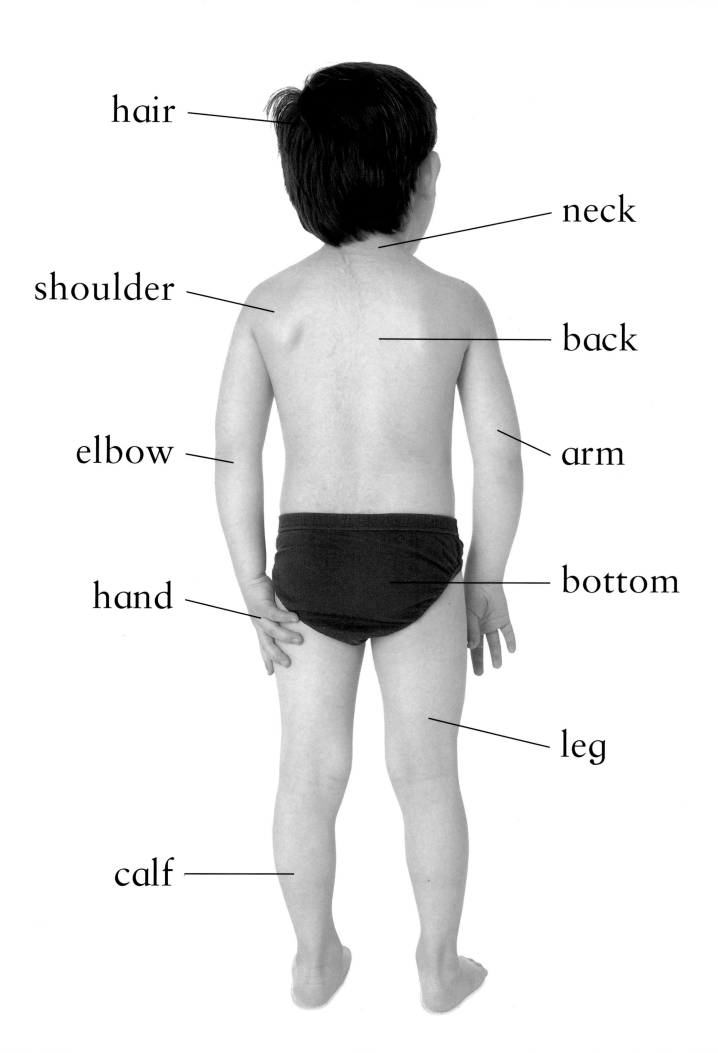

hair

neck

shoulder

back

elbow

arm

hand

bottom

leg

calf

Skin and Bones

skull

ribs

hip

ankle

Your body is covered in skin. Inside your body are bones. Your bones are joined together to make your skeleton.

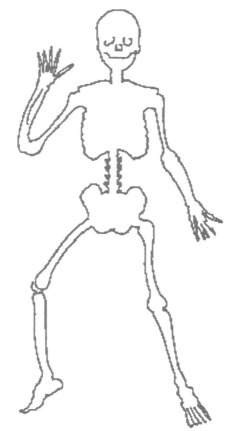

knuckles

kneecap

Without your skeleton, you would be a big blob!

See if you
can feel
these bones.
Press hard!

wrist   elbow   knee

Skin can
be dark...   light...

or freckled.

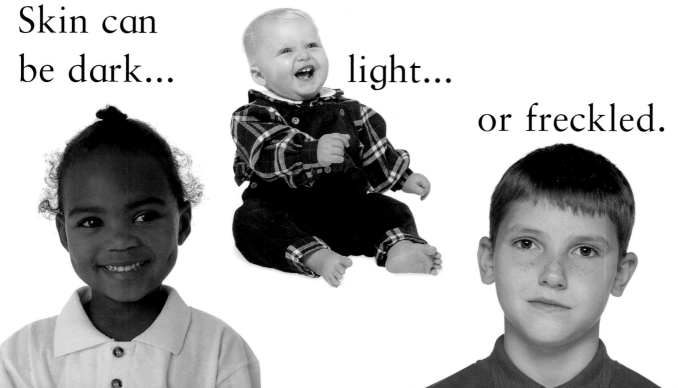

Mouth

Your mouth is for talking, eating and smiling!

You move your tongue and lips to talk.

lips

teeth

tongue

You use your teeth to take a bite of food.

You use your tongue to taste your food.

You use your mouth to...

smile

blow up a balloon

blow bubbles

After chewing your food, you swallow it.

lick an ice-cream cone

Eyes

You use your eyes to see all around you. When you are sad or hurt, tears fall from your eyes.

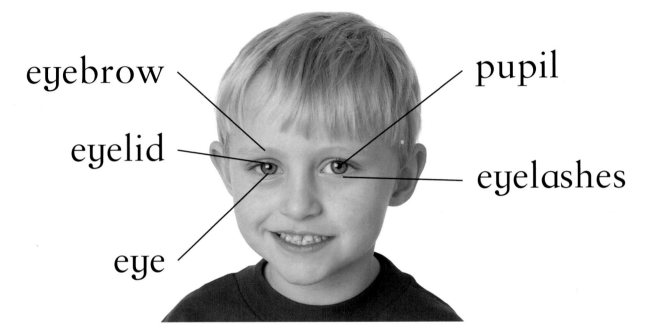

eyebrow

pupil

eyelid

eyelashes

eye

Eyes can be different colors. What color are your eyes?

blue eyes

brown eyes

You use
your eyes
to read.

Sunglasses
help us to
see in
bright
sunshine.

Glasses help eyes
to see better. Do
you wear glasses?

Can you
see my
eyes?

Nose

You use your nose to smell things. You sneeze through your nose, too.

nose

nostril

A-choo! Sometimes, sneezing means that you have a cold.

Flowers smell good.

When you have a cold, you blow your nose.

These animals use their noses to help them find food.

pig

dog

cat

Do these things smell good or bad?

pasta

herbs

onion

rose

perfume

Ears

You use your ears to hear all the noises around you.

ear

earlobe

What noises do these things make?

drum

bells

clapping

baby crying

cassette player

You use
your
ears to
listen to
stories...

and to
music...

or to hear
whispers.

Some people use a
hearing aid to help
their ears work better.

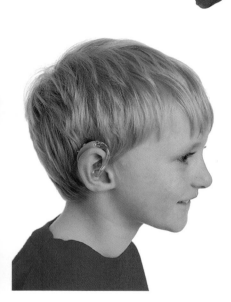

I'm shouting.
Can you
hear me?

earrings

earmuffs

Hair

Hair grows on
your body.

curly hair

short hair

long hair

straight hair

Hair can be different colors.

blonde
hair

brown
hair

black
hair

You need to brush your hair...

or comb it...

and have it cut.

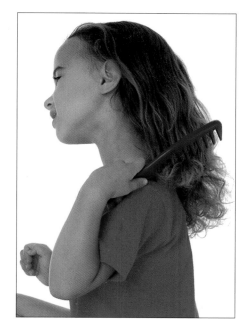

Babies do not have much hair.

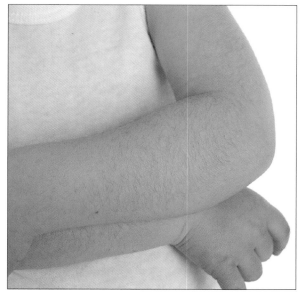

Your skin is covered with tiny hairs.

Hands

You use your hands to hold, feel and make things.

finger

palm

thumb

wrist

knuckle

nail

Do you draw with your left hand or your right hand?

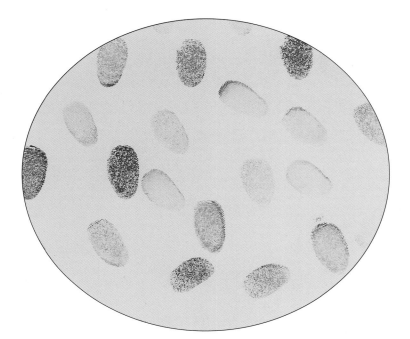

Everybody has different fingerprints. What are yours like?

Look at all
these things
your hands
help you do.
Can you
think of
some more?

catching

making
music

painting

cutting

cooking

Arms and Legs

Your arms and legs help you to walk, run, jump, dance and play games.

arms

Which of these things can you do?

legs

stretching   throwing   jumping

dancing

cycling

jumping
rope

standing
on one
leg

hopping

Faces

Faces show how we are feeling.

I feel very
sleepy.

I feel very angry.
I am frowning.

I feel happy.
I am smiling.

I am
laughing
and feel
happy.

I feel upset.
I am crying.

I feel very sad.
I might cry.

Babies

Babies grow up into adults.

Babies play with toys.

They drink milk.

They sleep in cribs until they are bigger.

Babies wear
diapers.

They wear
small clothes.

They need
lots of food
to grow.

Growing

Baby clothes
are very small.

You grow too big
for your clothes.

Little boys grow
into bigger boys.

fingernails

Your nails grow too. They have to be cut quite often.

toenails

Little girls grow into bigger girls.

Growing Up

babies

Babies grow up into children.

children

Children
grow up
into
teenagers.

Teenagers grow
up into adults.

Can you name these parts of the body?

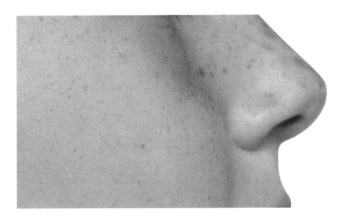

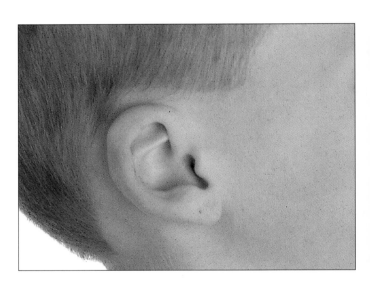

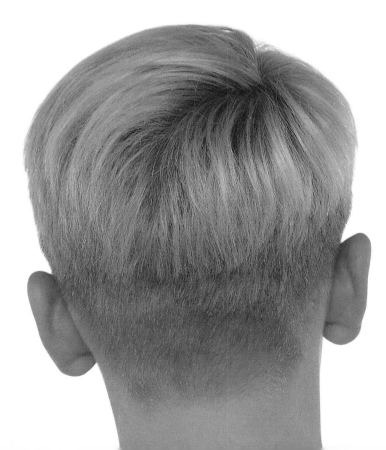

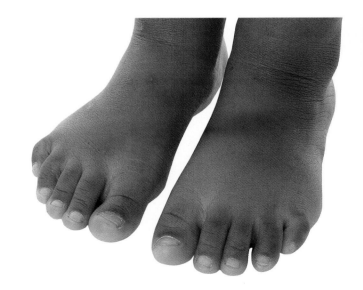

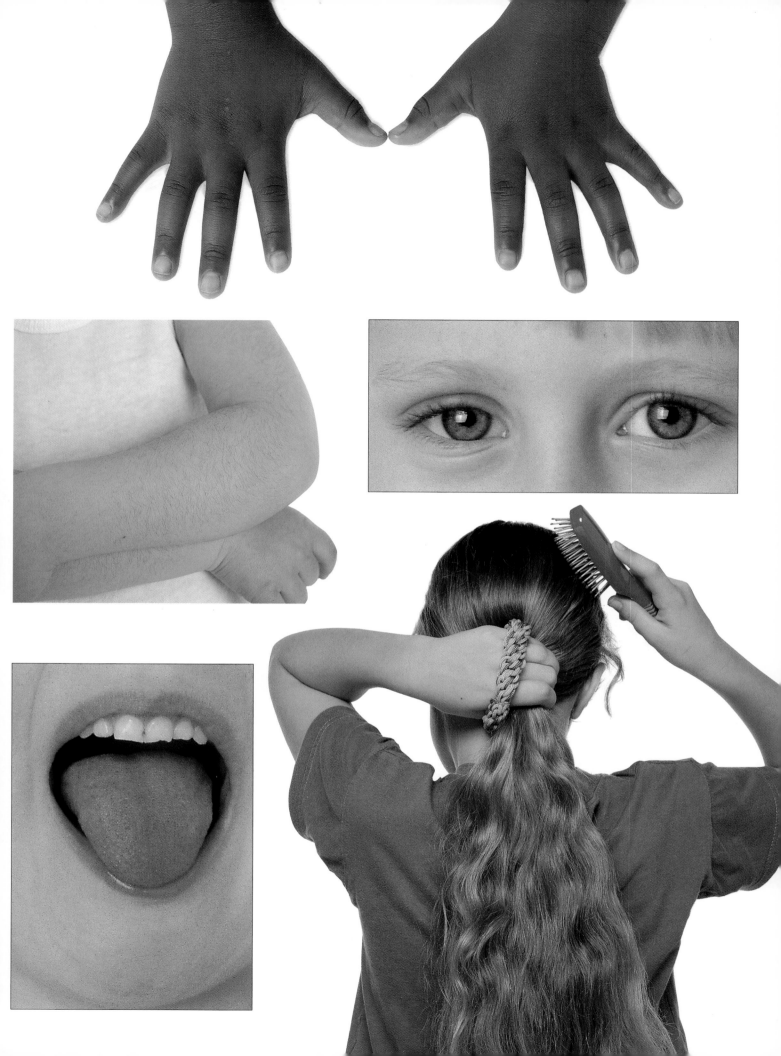

My Day

Waking Up

It's seven o'clock.
It's time to wake up.

Wake up,
teddy.

Wake up,
everyone.

I'm awake.

We're
awake.

I'm awake.

Getting Dressed

It's eight o'clock. It's time to get dressed.

What should I wear today?

red sweater and striped pants

red T-shirt

striped
T-shirt

blue
sweater
and blue
pants

Which ones
should I wear?

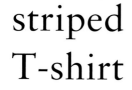

Now for
my shoes.

Having Breakfast

It's nine o'clock.
It's time for
breakfast.

I'm having
milk for
breakfast.

I'm having
cereal.

I'm having
toast and
jam.

orange
juice

bowls

apple juice

cup

Yum, that
was good.

yogurt

Painting

It's ten o'clock.
It's time to have some fun.

We're painting.

Do you like my painting?

paintbox

crayons

We're
drawing.

I can
paint too.

Going to the Park

It's eleven o'clock.
It's time to go to the park.

Teddy likes to jump rope too.

At the park I can use my jump rope.

Wheee! Down the slide!

Teddy likes
the swing too.

It's fun on
the swing.

Teddy likes to
ride on my bike.

Party Time

It's twelve o'clock.
It's time to go to
a party.

party
hat

gifts

What's in here?

balloon

What a mess!

Lunch

It's one o'clock.
It's lunchtime.

Let's make
lunch.

I'm having
yogurt.

I'm
eating
pizza.

What's for dessert?

ice
cream
sundae

fruit

I've
got an
ice
cream
cone...

or shall
I eat an
apple?

Playtime

It's two o'clock.
Let's play.

I'm building
a big palace.

I'm building
a tower.

Oh no...

I'm doing
a jigsaw
puzzle...

...and now
I'm playing
the xylophone.

I'm
playing
the
triangle.

Tea Party

It's three o'clock.
Teatime for toys.

We're having
a tea party.

More
cake,
teddy?

We like
strawberries...

and jelly...

and cakes.

More tea,
teddy?

Reading

It's four o'clock.

Big sister is back from school.

Let's read a book.

Teddy bears
like to hear
stories.

Do you want to read?

I'm
reading too.

So am I.

Supper Time

It's five o'clock.
Time for supper.

We're eating
pizza.

We're eating spaghetti.

What a mess!

Bath Time

It's six o'clock.
Time to have a bath.

ducks

Splash!

I have toys
and bubbles
in my bath.

I'm washing
my hair...

and cleaning
my face.

Time to
dry off.

Bedtime

It's seven o'clock.
It's time for bed.

We're in our
pajamas.

I'm going
to brush
my teeth.

Here's a snack.

I'm tired.

Everyone's asleep.

What time is it?

Is it
playtime?

Is it lunchtime?

Is it time to get up?

Is it time
for bed?

Is it five
o'clock?

Is it one
o'clock?

Is it eleven
o'clock?

Is it two
o'clock?

Is it nine
o'clock?

Is it six
o'clock?

Is it three
o'clock?

Is it seven
o'clock?

Is it twelve
o'clock?

My Home

The Kitchen

Food is stored and cooked in the kitchen.

vegetables

colander

cooker

oven mitt

saucepans

wastebasket

rolling pin

apron

wooden spoons

spatula

lemon squeezer

ladle

knives

frying pan

Refrigerator

Some foods need to be kept cold to stay fresh.

butter

yogurt

Look at all this food. It needs to go in the refrigerator.

cheese

sardines

chicken

milk

Freezer

Some foods have to be kept frozen. They go in the freezer.

fish sticks

Frozen french fries

peas

ice cubes

ice-cream cone

Cooking

Food is cooked in the kitchen.

cake pan

eggs, sugar and butter

whisk

baking sheet

We are making cupcakes.

What a mess!

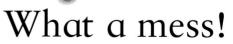

Cleaning up

There are lots of things to help us clean the kitchen.

dishcloth

brush

scouring pad

liquid soap

rag

I'm drying the dishes.

mop

bucket

Cupboard

Glasses, plates and food are kept in the cupboard.

jars

cans

cookie tin

bottles

I'll put this away.

carton

tea

cups

mugs

bowls

plates

saucers

I'm carrying glasses.

glasses

The Dining Room

The dining room is a special place for eating meals.

water pitcher

spoon

knife

fork

Eating lunch together.

napkin

We're hungry.

bread board

bread

fruit

What's for lunch?

place mat

Baby's Room

Sometimes babies sleep in a room of their own.

mobile

teddy

crib

I'm awake!

bottle

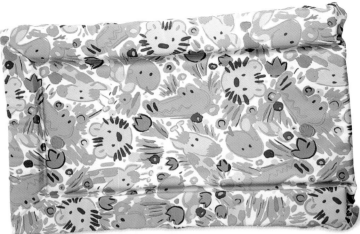

changing mat

blanket

It's playtime

diaper

wipes

sleeping bag

The Bathroom

toy boats

The bathroom is where we wash ourselves.

toothpaste

towel

toothbrush

hairbrush

soap

duck

mirror

I'm nice and clean.

bath

toilet

shampoo

toilet paper

potty

The Sitting Room

The sitting room is a comfortable place to relax.

coffee table

rug

bookshelves

story books

table
lamp

potted
plant

cushion

bean bag

photograph

pretty
flowers

The Playroom

jigsaw puzzle

You can paint, draw or play
with your toys in a playroom.

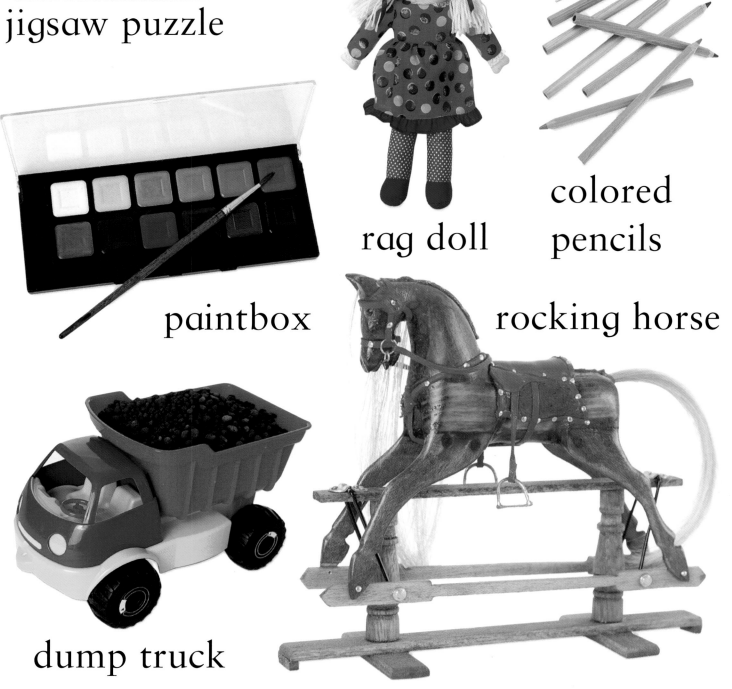

paintbox

rag doll

colored
pencils

rocking horse

dump truck

playhouse

tea set

coat rack

train
set

hand
puppet

chalk

I'm playing on my own.

The Bedroom

The bedroom is where you go to sleep and get dressed.

bookshelves

toys

clock

robes

slippers

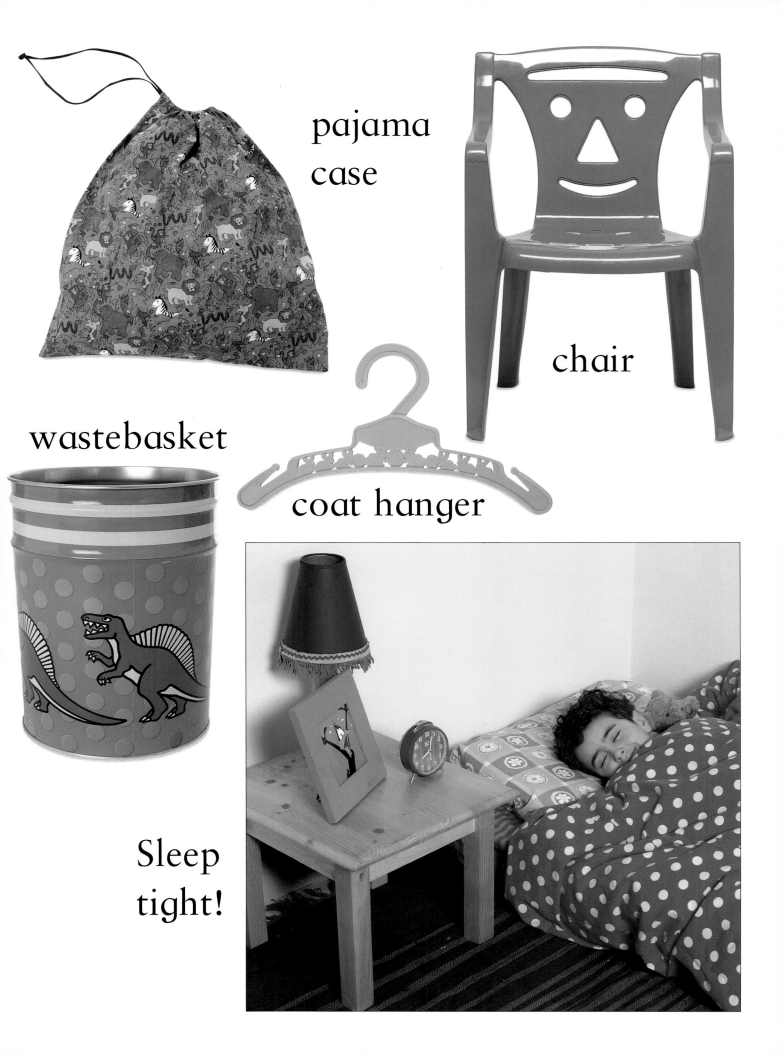

pajama case

chair

wastebasket

coat hanger

Sleep tight!

In the Garden

Lots of people grow
flowers in the garden.

seeds

soil

trowel

garden
wire

watering
can

broom

I'm
gardening.

Watering
the plants.

wheelbarrow

flowerpots

Picking
flowers.

flowers

The Toolshed

The toolshed is full of tools for grown-ups to use in the home.

cans of paint

rough sandpaper

hand
saw

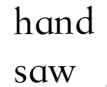

copper
nails

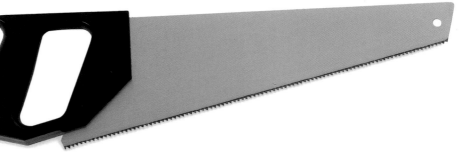

strong
rope

silver nails

screwdriver

hammer

nut

bolts

Fixing things with toy tools.

step ladder

Tidying Up

There are lots of things to help us tidy up our home.

Watch out!

What a mess!

I'll help.

Where do I start?

dustpan
and brush

feather
duster

broom

That's
better.

Where do they go?

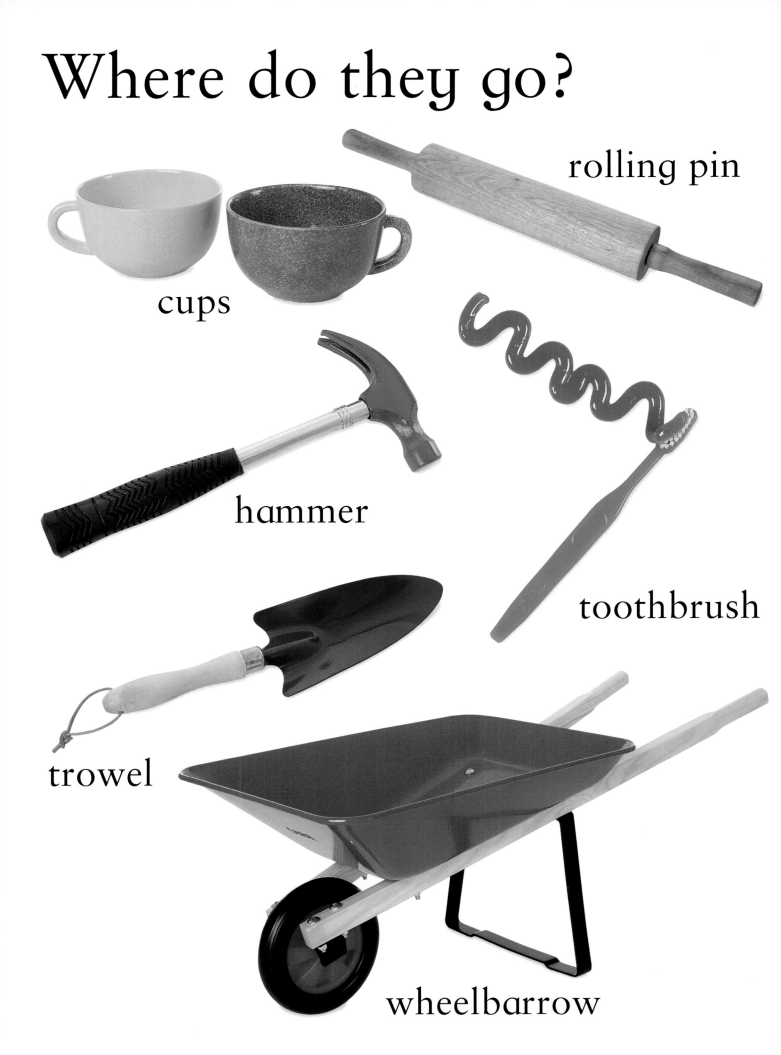

rolling pin

cups

hammer

toothbrush

trowel

wheelbarrow

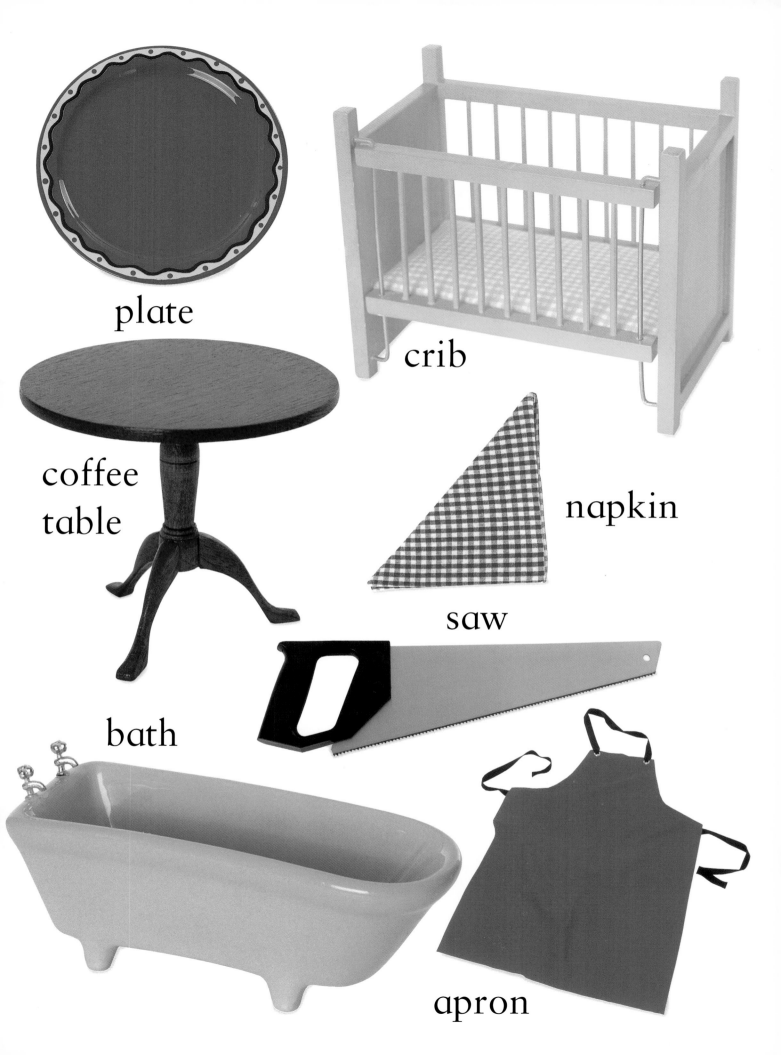

plate

crib

coffee table

napkin

saw

bath

apron

Acknowledgments

The publishers would like to thank the following children for modeling for this series of books:

Rosie Anness, Daisy Bartel, Chilli Bernstein, Caspian Broad, Karl Bolger, Lee Bolger, April Cain, Milo Clare, Tayah Ettienne, Matthew Ferguson, Africa George, Safari George, Safron George, Jamie Grant, Jack Harvey-Holt, Max Harvey-Holt, Faye Harrison, Zoe Harrison, Erin Hoel, Alice Jenkins, Kathleen Jenkins, Becky Johnson, Zamour Johnson, Rebekah Murrell, Amber McLaren, Nell Nixon, Tiffani Ogilvie, Giovanni Sipiano, Guiseppe Sipiano and Ella Wilks-Harper.